Little Book of
Soup

Collins

Little Book of
Soup

Introduction by
Hugh Fearnley-Whittingstall

With recipes from Nigella Lawson,
Jamie Oliver and Gordon Ramsay

Edited by **Annabel Buckingham** and **Thomasina Miers**

First published in 2006 by Collins,
an imprint of HarperCollinsPublishers
77–85 Fulham Palace Road
Hammersmith
London w6 8jb

The Collins website address is www.collins.co.uk

Collins is a registered trademark of HarperCollins Publishers Ltd

012	011	010	09	08	07	06
7	6	5	4	3	2	1

Text © various contributors 2006
Introduction © Hugh Fearnley-Whittingstall 2006
Photography © Richard Learoyd 2006

Design: George Lewis
Photographer: Richard Learoyd
Editor: Susan Fleming

Material in this book was previously published in *Soup Kitchen*

A catalogue record for this book is available from the British Library

ISBN–13 978-0-00-724301-3
ISBN–10 0-00-724301-4

Colour reproduction by Colourscan, Singapore
Printed and bound by Printing Express, Hong Kong

Contents

Foreword

Introduction by
Hugh Fearnley-Whittingstall

Foreword

Our book *Soup Kitchen* was the result of a year's work and an incredible journey. The motivation behind the book of soups was to raise money for the varied and wonderful work of homeless charities across the UK through the talents of a fantastic collection of chefs. We were somewhat cautious about taking it on but right from the start we both felt a tremendous excitement about making it happen. When we got on the phone to talk to chefs about soup, the results amazed even optimists like us. Within a week we had 12 recipes, by the next we had 40. Friends rallied round to share pearls of wisdom and outstanding professionals including a photographer, a graphic designer, law firm, literary agent, accountancy firm and website design company offered to work with us for free.

Soup Kitchen has sold very well, raising invaluable funds in the process, and is still going strong. We thought it would be fun to offer a second helping, however, in the form of this bite-sized selection of soups. As before, royalties benefit homeless charities including the Salvation Army and Centrepoint. We hope you'll enjoy cooking from it as much as we've enjoyed creating it.

Annabel and Tommi
www.soupkitchen.org.uk

Introduction by
Hugh Fearnley-Whittingstall

What is soup? Clearly it takes many forms. From a snack or a starter to a full blown supper, from a delicate but intense transparent infusion, to something so thick and robust you might want to swap your spoon for a knife and fork. Really, there is no more versatile dish on the planet. This explains soup's unique ability to cut across all the cultural boundaries of food, and delight the palates of men, women and children wherever they gather to share food.

Soup not only thrills the taste buds of diners the world over, it also stretches the imagination, and mediates the feelings, of all who love to cook. Sometimes it's a blend of subtle and extravagant ingredients fine tuned by a maverick genius to whet the appetite of a millionaire – for another seven courses to come. And sometimes it's a gloriously homey mix of vegetables, meat and seasoning served up by a devoted mother to a bickering family who may pause, almost imperceptibly and without self-awareness, to taste her love before resuming the fight. In both cases – in almost all cases – soup is demonstrative, honest, guileless, and dearly appreciated.

More prosaically, but importantly, soups are generally very healthy too. So often based on an encouraging, upbeat mix of fresh vegetables (with the protein element more of a spice than a staple) they are invariably enjoyed by those who may be sceptical of the same ingredients presented in a less heart-warming manner. They are therefore a brilliant way to ensure the bodies of our loved ones are getting the vitamins and minerals they need.

Soups naturally lend themselves to the undeniable virtues of sourcing locally, and cooking seasonally. In fact, one of your best options for creating

a quick and rewarding meal is to reach for three or four fresh seasonal vegetables, wash and prepare them as appropriate, and simmer them in some well-seasoned stock. Such a naturally improvised soup is rarely anything less than a pleasure. And with the addition of a little chopped leftover meat, some lentils or beans perhaps, pasta or rice, some toasted or fried bread croûtons, maybe a bit of grated cheese (really any, some, or all of these things), you are well into the realms of deep comfort and total satisfaction.

And soups are mostly excellent value for money. Leftovers are rich pickings, so that food that might otherwise go to waste can be reincarnated–often in a form that transcends the original. This means you can be magnanimous to your family and friends, even with meagre resources. They are also surprisingly portable, being able to travel almost anywhere you might consider taking a mug or flask of tea or coffee. You can eat soup at your desk at work, in front of the telly, on a bus or a boat, on a picnic (especially under a brolly in the rain).

As you will doubtless find as you explore the recipes in this book, soups are easy to make. This collection has been put together with contributions from the most talented and inspired chefs and cooks working in Britain today. Most of them are, if they put their minds to it, quite capable of baffling you with obscure ingredients and frustrating you with demanding techniques. But they won't do so here. Soup confounds attempts to be arcane or vainglorious in the kitchen. It finds even top flight cooks at their most relaxed and informal. The recipes in this collection are for the finest soups of the finest chefs. But they are easy going, down to earth and very, very do-able.

So please, like me, make this a working cookbook in a busy kitchen. Get it a bit soupy. Approach the recipes without fear. In fact, you could do a lot worse than bear in mind the well-chosen words of Fergus Henderson, from the introduction to his lovely book, *Nose to Tail Eating*:

"Do not be afraid of cooking as your ingredients will know, and misbehave. Enjoy your cooking and the food will behave; moreover it will pass your pleasure on to those who eat it."

Perhaps a good way of summarising the numerous and considerable virtues of soup is to say that it is always among the most generous and friendly of dishes. And that is why it has been chosen as the subject of a book with the most generous and friendly of intentions. The editors, Annabel and Thomasina, have put this collection together with the aim of raising much-needed funds for the homeless. Their amazing energy and enthusiasm, and inexhaustible optimism for the project, have been inspiring. In wholehearted support of this venture, every chef has given their time and contribution for free. This spirit of giving, above all things, forms the essence of the collection.

So we hope you too will be generous with this book, as with your soup-making. Buy a few extra copies, and dish them out. They're sure to slip down a treat.

Vegetable Stock

There are many versions of vegetable stock, but this one is quite gutsy.

Makes about 1.5 litres
2 large onions, studded with a few cloves, cut in chunks
4 carrots, cut in chunks
3 celery stalks, cut into chunks
1 fennel bulb, sliced
4 cabbage leaves, chopped
2 leeks, washed and roughly chopped
1 bouquet garni (see below)
zest of 1 lemon
5 black peppercorns
2 litres water

Put all the ingredients in a stockpot and bring to a simmer. Simmer for a couple of hours, topping up with water as needed, so the ingredients are always covered.
   Strain, cool and use! Or freeze.

Note
A bouquet garni is a bunch of herbs used to flavour soups and sauces. A bouquet normally consists of parsley, thyme and a few dried bay leaves, but can be adapted as creatively as you wish. Normally tied together in a bundle so that the herbs don't escape, and so that they can be deftly removed just before serving (unless you buy the little, ready-prepared sachets from grocers or supermarkets). NB If you are making your own bouquet, never be tempted to use an elastic band to tie it together it will leave a horrible, plastic flavour to your broth. String is much more advisable (but not blue).

Chicken Stock

Probably the most useful of all kinds of stock, a chicken stock will add flavour to anything from a sauce to a risotto or stew and, of course, many soup recipes, provided you are not cooking for vegetarians. If it is really well made you can drink it neat too. The most obvious way to make a chicken stock is by using the bones and leftovers from a roast, but if you are making a stock from a fresh, raw chicken, just throw the chicken in a 180ºC/Gas 4 oven for 15 minutes to brown it a little and get a bit of flavour in your stock. If you are using a leftover carcass, adding a raw neck of chicken, or gizzard, and some giblets will add to the flavour and depth. If you want a stronger stock, simmer to reduce. You will have less liquid than designated below, but it will have a richer flavour.

Makes 1–1.5 litres, depending on size of pot and bird
1 cooked chicken carcass, with all the leftover
gunk (skin, fat, jelly, ooze)
1 large onion, or 2 medium, with a few cloves
stuck in, cut in chunks
2 carrots, cut in chunks
2 celery stalks, cut in chunks
3 black peppercorns
1 bouquet garni (see page 12)
2 garlic cloves (optional)

Put all the ingredients in a large pot (big enough to fit ingredients, but with not much spare room), and cover with water. Bring to a gentle simmer and simmer for up to 5 hours, but no longer, or leave in a very low warm oven overnight (100ºC). Skim away any grey scum as it comes to the surface (which contain impurities), and keep topping up with hot water as the water evaporates so that the goods are always covered.

Strain and cool, skimming off any fat that rises to the surface. Chill or freeze.

Beef Stock

Beef shin is particularly good in a beef stock, as are the ribs and leg. Bones are what give the rich, gelatinous feel we're searching for.

Makes about 1.5–2 litres depending on size of pot and timing

2.5kg beef bones
2 onions, unpeeled and quartered
2 carrots, chopped
2 leeks, washed and chopped
1 tbsp vegetable oil
1 bouquet garni (see page 12)
10 black peppercorns

Preheat the oven to 200ºC/Gas 6.

Wash the bones thoroughly and roast for half an hour with the onion until well browned.

Sauté the veggies in oil in the stockpot until taking up a bit of colour, and then add the bones and onion. Cover with water and add the bouquet garni and peppercorns. Cover with water and bring to the boil. Simmer gently for 3–5 hours, skimming off scum as it emerges, and topping up with hot water.

Strain well, the second time through a fine chinois, and cool. Refrigerate and skim off the fat. If you wish to freeze the stock, put back in a clean saucepan and simmer to reduce quantity, intensifying the flavour. Pour into a few ice-cube trays and freeze your home-made stock cubes.

Vegetables

Roast Pumpkin Soup with Crispy Garlic

I've always liked pumpkins and squashes made into a soup, and I love them roasted too. This year, thinking how delicious the flavours are that you get when you roast peppers and tomatoes, and what good soup that makes, I decided on a similar approach with my favourite squash varieties. The result was gorgeous. You can use any pumpkin or squash for this soup, and the ever-popular butternut works particularly well. But if you can get some of the other sweet squash varieties, such as sweet mama, acorn, or kabocha, generally available from mid-October to late November, then so much the better.

Serves 4
1 medium pumpkin or 2 small squashes
2 tbsp extra virgin olive oil, plus extra for garnish
6 garlic cloves, lightly crushed, plus a few extra for garnish
salt and pepper to taste
1 litre Chicken or Vegetable Stock (see pages 14 and 12)

Preheat the oven to 200ºC/Gas 6.

There's no need to peel the pumpkin or squashes. Just cut them into rough chunks or thick slices and scrape away the seeds and surrounding soft fibres. Lay the slices in a large roasting tin, and drizzle generously with olive oil. Scatter the garlic cloves, whole with the skin on, over the tray, and season well with salt and pepper.

Put in the preheated oven for 35–40 minutes, turning once or twice if you like, so the pumpkin pieces are well roasted and nicely browned. Use a spoon to scrape

the soft flesh of the roasted pumpkin pieces away from the skin. Heat the stock in a pan. Put some of the scraped flesh into a liquidiser, along with the flesh squeezed out from the roasted garlic cloves, and pour in enough hot stock to cover. Liquidise in batches, until completely smooth, returning the soup to a clean pan. Taste the soup and adjust the seasoning. Add enough stock to get a thick and creamy consistency.

Heat the soup through without re-boiling it, and as you are doing so, fry a few thin slivers of garlic in a little oil. Scatter these thin shards of crisp fried garlic over each bowl of hot soup as you serve it. Finish, if you like, with a trickle of olive oil.

Jill Dupleix   Cookery editor, The Times

Curried Sweet Potato Soup

This is my favourite sort of soup, one that just tastes sweetly of vegetables and not much else. It doesn't need chicken stock, as it makes its own sweet potato stock as it cooks. The white beans then give it a lush, velvety texture, and the curry powder makes it irresistible. I serve it in a big bowl with a great whacking slice of grilled sourdough bread sticking half in and half out of the bowl. It also dresses up nicely for dinner, with a dollop of soured cream or yoghurt, and some warm Indian naan bread on the side.

Serves 4

1kg orange-fleshed sweet potato
1.2 litres boiling water or stock (see pages 12–15)
salt and pepper to taste
400g canned white beans
1 tsp good curry powder, or more
2 tbsp fresh parsley or coriander leaves

Peel the sweet potatoes and cut into small cubes. Put in a pan, add the boiling water or stock, salt and pepper, and bring to the boil. Simmer for 15 minutes or until the sweet potato is soft.

Drain the beans and rinse. Add half the beans and the curry powder to the soup, stirring well, then whizz in a food processor in batches, being careful not to overfill the bowl.

Return to the pan, add the remaining whole beans, and gently heat. If too thick, add extra boiling water. Taste for salt, pepper and curry powder, and scatter with parsley or coriander.

Fergus Henderson St John, Clerkenwell, London

New Season Garlic and Bread Soup

This is a very simple, but reviving and steadying soup. For the early months of spring you can get fresh garlic before it is dried. It has a longer, greener stem, giving you the flavour of garlic with a youthful nature. A mouli is very useful for this recipe – in fact a mouli is useful all the time.

Serves 6

8 fresh whole garlic bulbs
1 litre Chicken Stock (see page 14)
salt and pepper to taste
a healthy handful of chunks, without crust, of
yesterday's – if not even the day before's – white bread

Place the garlic in the stock and bring to the boil, then reduce to a simmer until the garlic is cooked soft, approximately 40 minutes. Then pass the garlic through the mouli (if you have no mouli, press it through a sieve).

Mix the garlic pulp back into the stock and season to taste. Reheat and throw in the bread a couple of minutes before serving, so it has just long enough to sup up the soup but not fall apart.

Creamy Mushroom Soup

Serves 6

1kg flat mushrooms
2 large shallots, chopped
1 garlic clove, chopped
50g butter
1 litre Chicken Stock (see page 14)
500ml milk
100ml double cream
truffle oil to taste
salt and pepper to taste

Remove the gills from the mushrooms and chop the flesh up into quite large pieces. Sweat off the shallots and garlic in the butter until soft but before they have taken on any colour. Add the mushrooms and sweat down with the shallots and garlic.

Cover with the chicken stock and milk and simmer for about 20 minutes.

Blitz in a food processor, and pass through a sieve. Adjust the flavour and texture with the cream and extra milk if needed.

Season with truffle oil, salt and pepper, and serve with hot fresh bread (and some chopped parsley if you like).

Thomasina Miers

Winner, MasterChef

Tortilla Soup

This is a Mexican classic. It's simple, but at the same time sophisticated; it's easy to make yet creates a wow when you put it down on the table. You can make it with bits of leftover chicken for the perfect, comforting soup for hangovers or invalids, or you can make it as below for a lighter, more fragrant version. Either way you'll fall in love with it and make it again and again and again. I guarantee it!

Serves 4
1.2 litres chicken stock (see page 14)
1 onion, peeled and cut into 6 pieces
3 garlic cloves, peeled
1 x 400g can tomatoes or 4-6 fresh tomatoes,
skinned and seeded
6 corn tortillas
5 tbsp olive or vegetable oil
1-2 dried ancho chilli, stem and seeds removed
(see note below)
200g buffalo mozzarella or barrel-aged feta,
diced in ½cm pieces
1 large, ripe avocado, diced as with the cheese
1 large lime, cut into wedges

Put the onion and garlic in a large, heavy frying pan on a fairly hot flame, and dry toast for 5-6 minutes until they start to take on a golden colour, stirring regularly. Put them in a food processor or blender with the tomatoes and whiz to a purée.

Put the purée in a saucepan on a medium-high heat and reduce to a thick, tomato purée. Add the stock and simmer for 25 minutes. Season to taste, bearing in mind that feta is saltier than mozzarella. (This can be done the day before.)

Put the chilli in a dry frying pan and toast for 30 seconds – be careful not to burn it or the chilli will taste bitter. Tear into strips.

Cut the tortillas in half and then cut each half into 2 cm long strips. Heat the oil in a saucepan until shimmering (test with a tortilla strip to see if it sizzles which means the oil is hot enough). Add half the strips and fry, stirring constantly until the pieces are golden brown and crispy. Take out and dry on kitchen paper. Repeat with the remaining strips; you can re-use the oil for another recipe.

When you are ready to eat divide the tortilla strips and chilli strips between 4 bowls. Add the tomato broth. On the table arrange the cheese, avocado and lime wedges so that each person can add liberally to their soup, squeezing on the lime juice. You may also like to chop some flat leaf parsley or coriander to garnish (the Mexicans use a herb called epazote if you can find it).

Note
Several companies now supply Mexican chillies in this country, but if you can't get hold of ancho chillies, add a little smoked paprika to your broth and a little fresh chilli or even some strips of sun-dried tomato for a slightly different twist.

Cabbage Soup, Valtellina Style
Zuppa di Cavolo Valtellinense

What a wonderful (and economical) way of using leftover bread. Cabbage is cheap, too. The other ingredients are very typical of the Aosta Valley and make this remarkable, simple and delicious winter dish. Mmmmm.

Serves 4
675g Savoy cabbage
salt and pepper to taste
6 slices stale bread, cut into cubes
275g Fontina cheese, cut into small cubes
1 litre Chicken Stock (see page 14)
50g butter

Clean, trim and slice the cabbage. Boil in lightly salted water until tender, then drain. Place a large saucepan over a low heat. Put a layer of cabbage while still warm in the bottom, then a layer of bread, then a layer of Fontina cheese.

Continue doing this until the ingredients are finished. Gently press down the ingredients with the ladle. Bring the stock to the boil and pour over the other ingredients. Leave to soak for a couple of minutes.

Meanwhile, melt the butter in a small pan. While still foaming pour it over the soup. Stir and serve hot.

(From *Antonio Carluccio's Italian Feast*, BBC Books, 1996)

Gary Rhodes Rhodes Twenty Four, City, London

Pea Soup

Serves 4 (as a generous starter)
600ml water (stock could also be used, see pages 12–15)
450g podded peas (frozen can also be used)
salt and pepper to taste
a pinch of caster sugar
100ml whipping or single cream

Bring the water or stock to the boil in a saucepan and add the peas. Bring back to the boil and cook for 5 minutes until tender (longer if necessary). Remove from the heat, season with salt, pepper and a pinch of sugar, and liquidise to a smooth creamy soup.

For the smoothest of finishes, strain through a sieve. The soup at this stage can be cooled over ice to help maintain its colour then simply re-heated when needed.

If serving immediately, add the cream and return to a gentle simmer, seasoning once again with salt and pepper.

Note
For an added twist to this soup and to transform it into a tasty main course, ladle the soup around a pan-fried fillet of fresh cod topped with toasted sesame seeds and finished with a drop or two of sesame oil. A little chopped mint can be added to the soup, creating the classic pea and mint combination.

A sprinkling of flavoured stock cube (chicken or vegetable) can be added to the water, offering a slightly stronger finish to the soup.

Delia Smith Food writer

Cauliflower Soup with Roquefort

This is a truly sublime soup, as the cauliflower and Roquefort seem to meld together so well, but I have also tried it with mature Cheddar and I'm sure it would be good with any cheese you happen to have handy.

Serves 4–6

1 medium, good-sized cauliflower, about 570g
2 bay leaves
salt and pepper to taste
25g butter
1 medium onion, chopped
2 celery stalks, chopped
1 large leek, washed and chopped
110g potatoes, peeled and diced
2 tbsp half-fat crème fraîche
50g Roquefort cheese, crumbled, or mature Cheddar, grated
1 tbsp snipped fresh chives

The stock for this is very simply made with all the cauliflower trimmings. Trim the cauliflower into small florets and then take the stalk bits, including the green stems, and place these trimmings in a medium-sized saucepan. Then add 1.5 litres water, the bay leaves and some salt, bring to the boil and simmer for 20 minutes with a lid.

Meanwhile, take another large saucepan with a well-fitting lid. Melt the butter in it over a gentle heat, then add the onion, celery, leek and potato, cover and let the vegetables gently sweat for 15 minutes. Keep the heat very low, then when the stock is ready, strain it into the pan to join the vegetables, adding the bay leaves as well

but throwing out the rest. Now add the cauliflower florets, bring it all back up to simmering point and simmer very gently for 20–25 minutes, until the cauliflower is completely tender, this time without a lid.

After that, remove the bay leaves, then place the contents of the saucepan in a food processor or blender and process until the soup is smooth and creamy. Next return it to the saucepan, stir in the crème fraîche and cheese, and keep stirring until the cheese has melted and the soup is hot but not boiling. Check the seasoning, then serve in hot bowls, garnished with the chives.

Aubergine and Pepper Soup with Sautéed Cherry Tomatoes

Serves 4–6

4 medium aubergines
leaves from 1 sprig fresh rosemary
1 tbsp chopped garlic
olive oil, for frying
salt and pepper to taste
2 large red peppers
2 large yellow peppers
1 shallot, chopped
2 sprigs fresh basil
1 tbsp coarse-grain mustard
300ml Vegetable or Chicken Stock (see pages 12 and 14)
250ml tomato juice
200g cherry tomatoes on the vine

Preheat the oven to 190ºC/Gas 5.

Peel the skin from the aubergines in long strips using a swivel vegetable peeler, taking about 5mm of the flesh still attached to the skin. Cut the skin into long strips and then into small dice. Set aside.

Wrap the peeled aubergines in foil with the rosemary leaves and garlic. Roast for about 45 minutes or until the flesh has completely broken and softened. Save the cooking juices.

Heat about 2 tbsp olive oil in a large frying pan and, when hot, cook the soft aubergine flesh over a high heat to give it a slightly scorched flavour. Mix in the saved roasting juices and season. Remove from the pan and set aside to cool. Stand the peppers upright on the board and cut the flesh from the central seed core and stalk. Chop the pepper flesh.

Add another tbsp or two of oil to the frying pan and, when hot, sauté the shallot until lightly coloured. Mix in the peppers and continue frying over a high heat for about 5 minutes. Mix in the basil and mustard, and then the stock. Bring to the boil and season, then simmer for 12–15 minutes. Remove from the heat and cool.

Discard the basil, then pour the pepper mixture into a food processor or blender. Add the aubergine and whizz until creamy and smooth. The soup will be quite thick. Gradually mix in the tomato juice. Chill until ready to serve.

To prepare the garnish, heat a little oil in the frying pan and fry the reserved chopped aubergine until light and crisp. Drain on kitchen paper.

Pull the tomatoes from the stalks and fry them in a little more oil to flavour the skin. They will go a bit squashy, which is fine. Drain on kitchen paper.

Check the seasoning of the soup then pour into 4–6 chilled serving bowls. Divide the sautéed tomatoes among the bowls and scatter over the aubergine flakes.

From *A Chef for All Seasons*, Gordon Ramsay, Quadrille, 2000

Mark Hix   The Ivy, Covent Garden, London

Iced Plum Tomato Soup with Basil and Mozzarella

This eternally popular soup wasn't originally made for the restaurant at all: it was a staple of the outside catering business. We must have served it a thousand times before it finally got put on the menu. It was an immediate success. It is a simple dish to make but do not be tempted to use anything other than ripe plum tomatoes or other well-flavoured ones. It is an intensely flavoured soup and therefore served in small quantities.

Serves 4–6

500g soft plum tomatoes, halved and seeded
500g cherry tomatoes
300ml tomato juice
3 tsp balsamic vinegar
1 garlic clove, blanched in water for 2 minutes
salt and pepper to taste

Garnish

150g mozzarella cheese (baby ones if possible), sliced
60ml basil and olive oil purée (simply blitz together), or pesto
a handful of small basil leaves (purple if possible)
150g mixed tomatoes, cherry, yellow, plum etc., cut into small pieces

Process the plum tomatoes in a blender with the cherry tomatoes, tomato juice, balsamic vinegar and garlic, and pass the mixture through a fine sieve. Correct the seasoning to taste, adding a little more balsamic vinegar if necessary.

Chill the soup in the freezer for 20–30 minutes. Serve in a soup plate with small slices of mozzarella, basil purée, small basil leaves, and a selection of tomato pieces.

Asparagus Soup

I always look forward to those 6 weeks from the middle of May until the end of June with great excitement, heralding the arrival of Norfolk asparagus. I'm sure other counties will say the same, but I reckon Norfolk asparagus is the best, and this recipe is born from all the trimmings left when preparing asparagus the way we do at Morston Hall... And of course, being a proprietor, I hate wasting anything.

Serves 8–10

3 large bunches Norfolk asparagus
125g salted butter
1 large onion, thinly sliced
1 small potato, thinly sliced
1.2 litres Chicken or Vegetable Stock (see pages 14 or 12)
175g spinach leaves
150ml double cream
salt and pepper to taste

Cut the asparagus tips off so they are about the length of your middle finger. Lightly peel the bottom 2.5cm towards the cut end to create a neat white stalk and a plump green top. Retain the peelings. Chop the stalks and add to the peelings.

In a large pan, melt 55g of the butter over a medium heat, then add the sliced onion and potato. In another saucepan heat the stock. Once the onions and potatoes are soft, add the asparagus stalks and trimmings, and pour in the hot stock. Bring to the boil and simmer until the stalks are tender. Meanwhile, blanch the asparagus tips in boiling salted water for about 3 minutes, then drain and refresh in cold water.

When ready to serve, fry briefly in 15g of the remaining butter.

Take the soup pot off the heat, add the spinach and whizz up in a liquidiser or food processor. Finally, push through a fine sieve: the easiest way to do this, I find, is with the back of a ladle.

Just before serving, bring the soup back up to temperature, add the remaining butter and the cream, and check the seasoning.

Serve topped with the blanched, buttered asparagus tips and, if you like, a thin strip of crispy streaky bacon.

Meat

Chestnut and Chorizo Soup/Sopa de Castañas

Forests of sweet chestnut thrive in the mountainous regions of Spain. This recipe combines some of the classic flavours of Spanish cooking to produce a warm, comforting and mildly spicy soup that is synonymous with the onset of autumn.

Serves 4

4 tbsp olive oil
1 large Spanish onion, diced
1 medium carrot, diced
1 celery stalk, thinly sliced
120g mild cooking chorizo, cut into 1cm cubes
salt and pepper to taste
2 garlic cloves, thinly sliced
1 tsp ground cumin
1½ tsp finely chopped fresh thyme leaves
2 small dried red chillies, crushed
2 tomatoes, fresh or tinned, roughly chopped
500g cooked peeled chestnuts (fresh or vacuum packed), roughly chopped
20 saffron strands, infused in 3-4 tbsp boiling water
1 litre water

In a large saucepan, heat the oil over a medium heat. Add the onion, carrot, celery, chorizo and a pinch of salt and fry for about 20 minutes, stirring occasionally, until

everything caramelises and turns quite brown. This gives the soup a wonderfully rich colour and taste.

Now add the garlic, cumin, thyme and chilli and cook for 1 more minute, followed by the tomato and, after about 2 minutes, the chestnuts. Give everything a good stir, then add the saffron-infused liquid and the water, and simmer for about 10 minutes.

Remove from the heat and mash by hand (with a potato masher) until almost smooth but still with a little bit of texture. Season with salt and pepper.

(From *Moro The Cookbook*, Ebury Press, 2001)

Stracciatella with Fresh Chicken

This soup was served in Australian restaurants in the late 1980s when the chef was too lazy to make a slow-cooked soup for the daily menu, or an underling forgot. It is, however, one of the most delicious and simple soups you could ever eat, even easier now that fresh stocks are readily available on the supermarket shelves, if you don't want to make your own. And, if push comes to shove, you can use a stock cube. The important thing with this soup is to take it from the heat as soon as you have added the egg mix or it will overcook. The egg, Parmesan and parsley will float to the top like a raft, leaving the rich stock and chunks of chicken sitting below.

Serves 6

1.5 litres Chicken Stock (see page 14)
3 skinless chicken breasts, cut into strips
4 eggs
60g Parmesan, freshly grated
a good handful of parsley, finely chopped
ground black pepper to taste

Place a suitable saucepan over a high heat, pour in the stock and bring to the boil. Add the chicken to the boiling stock, and cook for 5 minutes.

Beat the eggs with the cheese, chopped parsley and black pepper.

Pour the egg mix into the boiling liquid and remove from the heat immediately.

Serve in 6 large bowls, with crusty bread and butter or olive oil.

Roast Chicken, Wild Mushroom and Onion Soup

Probably serves about 4 really greedy bastards (or 8 nancies) as a starter.

Joint a chicken, divide the legs and drummers into two, and chop up the carcass. In a big cast-iron pan, brown the pieces in butter (but not the breasts) together with the carcass (and ideally a pig's trotter if you happen to have one – if you are Jewish, you may not). Season the chicken really well. When the chicken is really dark golden, remove and reserve.

In the same pan reserve a little fat and sweat 3 finely sliced (not chopped) onions with 2–3 garlic cloves until well caramelised – this will take at least half an hour. Keep scraping the pan as you go to prevent catching, and then season the onions. When softened and caramelised, add half a bottle of white wine or dry cider and boil down until nearly all the liquid has evaporated.

Add back the chicken pieces and carcass and cover with ideally chicken stock (or water). Throw in a couple of bay leaves and a big bunch of thyme. When the soup comes to a very gentle simmer, skim well twice.

Cook very gently for about an hour, then fish out the chicken pieces and carcass; throw out the carcass and the trotter, if used. Discard the herbs too.

Sauté the chicken breasts really well, skin-side down, so they go a nice dark golden colour. Deglaze your sauté pan with a splash of soup and return both (i.e. breasts and the residue from the sauté pan) back to the soup. Skim the soup again.

Sauté a generous pan of wild mushrooms (whatever is around, buttons are also good, but you will need plenty), season well and drain after cooking. Throw the mushrooms (the more the merrier) into the soup.

Serve when the chicken breasts are cooked: they take very little time – about 10 minutes at a very gentle simmer. (On no account boil them or they will end up dry.)

Take out the breasts and carve each into 3 pieces.

Delicious. Adjust the seasoning, stir in a handful of chopped fresh tarragon and flat parsley, and serve at once with crusty bread. Or with some gnocchi or noodles as a tasty lunch.

Nigella Lawson Food writer

Yellow Split Pea and Frankfurter Soup

The glorious golden yellowness of the soup makes it a suitable marker for the New Year, implying, as it does, a hope for golden times ahead. I felt, too, the split peas themselves were a kind of northern European take on the Italian custom of serving lentils for their coin-like appearance.

But the value of this soup is so much more than symbolic, important though that is in festive eating particularly. The grainy liquid is hearty on its own, and the best way of soaking up excess alcohol – or after-effects of same – lingering in the system. The frankfurters, again to be sliced in coins if you want to play further on this theme, or cut in thick slices otherwise, make this a real meal and a half.

Serves 6–8
1 onion
1 carrot
1 garlic clove
1 celery stalk
2–3 tbsp vegetable oil
½ tsp ground mace
500g yellow split peas
1.25–1.5 litres Chicken or Vegetable Stock (see pages 14 or 12)
2 bay leaves
approx. 8 frankfurters

Peel the onion, carrot and garlic and cut the onion and carrot into rough chunks. Put them all, along with the roughly cut-up celery, into the bowl of a food processor. Blitz until all are finely chopped.

Spoon the oil into a heavy-based wide saucepan and put on a medium heat. When warm, add the chopped vegetables from the processor and cook for 5–10 minutes, until soft but not coloured.

Add the ground mace – this may be a small amount but it's crucial to the taste – give a good stir and then add the split peas and stir again till they're glossily mixed with the oil-slicked, cooked-down vegetables. Pour over 1.25 litres stock and add the bay leaves, then bring to the boil. Cover, turn down the heat and cook for about an hour until everything is tender and sludgy, adding more stock as needed. Sometimes the peas seem to thicken too much before they actually cook and need to be watered down. Taste for seasoning once everything's ready.

You can add the frankfurters as you wish. It's probably easiest just to cut them into slices – I tend to add them in chunks of about 3cm each – and throw them into the soup to warm, but I just put them into the microwave (40 seconds on high is about right for one or two franks; fiddle about with times when there are more), then slice them hot and add them to each person's bowl as they come. Not an elegant soup, I'll admit, but a near-perfect one.

(From *Feast*, Nigella Lawson, Chatto & Windus, 2004)

EAT - Hungarian Goulash

Hungry and cold on the ramparts of the Hohensalzburg Fortress in Salzburg with my husband on a snowy winter's evening in 1989, talking too loudly in English about a hot meal, preferably of goulash, we were accosted by a smartly dressed couple who invited us - without preamble - to come to their home and...eat goulash!

So off we went to enjoy the wonderful hospitality of this generous, food-loving couple in their warm Salzburg kitchen. Perfect!

Traditional goulash, it transpired, is made without any water at all. Equal amounts of onion and beef left to simmer will generate all the liquid required for this dish. The simplicity impressed us and we resolved, some seven years later when we started EAT, to make a Hungarian goulash soup along the same lines. Adding some stock to attain the consistency needed for soup felt rather blasphemous but it works and we love this recipe - as do our customers.

EAT is a small company dedicated to quality food. We believe in simplicity, honesty and using real ingredients - hence our name The Real Food Company. Our soups are all cooked in our own kitchen to our own recipes much as you would at home, with lots of chopping, dicing, stirring and simmering.

We love fresh, delicious hot soup and are constantly inspired by people like our Salzburg friends with a passion for food.

Serves 6

700g beef chuck steak, cut into 2.5cm (1in) cubes
700g onions (about 5), diced
2 tbsp olive oil
2 heaped tbsp sweet Hungarian paprika
½ tsp whole caraway seeds
250g tomatoes, chopped
750ml Beef Stock (see page 15)
3 large potatoes, peeled and cut into large dice
salt and pepper to taste
chopped fresh flat-leaf parsley

Heat the oil over high heat (best in a heavy cast-iron pot). Sear the chuck steak in small batches to ensure a nice rich colour and then set aside.

In the same pot sauté the diced onions in the olive oil, stirring until they begin to colour, then lower the heat and cover, letting them sweat until soft.

When the onions are soft, add the paprika, caraway, tomato, seared beef and beef stock. Cover and let simmer for at least an hour until the meat becomes very tender. Add the cubed potatoes and cook another half-hour until tender. Season with salt and pepper to taste.

Serve nice and hot with a sprinkling of chopped parsley.

Pulses & Pasta

Chickpea, Leek and Parmesan Soup

Serves 4
2 medium leeks
15g butter
2 garlic cloves, chopped
1 handful fresh thyme, leaves picked
1 x 400g can chickpeas, drained and rinsed
600ml Chicken Stock (see page 14)
2 medium potatoes, peeled and chopped
salt and pepper to taste
extra virgin olive oil
freshly grated Parmesan

Trim the outside of the leeks back then cut off any coarse green tops and discard them. Cut the leeks in half lengthways and slice the halves into fine shreds. Put the chopped leeks in a colander and rinse thoroughly under running water, removing any dirt.

In a large saucepan, gently heat the butter and add the garlic, leeks and thyme leaves. Put the lid on the pot and slowly cook until soft without colouring.

Add the chickpeas to the leeks with the chicken stock and potatoes. Bring to the boil then simmer gently for half an hour or so or until the potatoes are well cooked. If the soup is too thick, loosen it with a little boiling water.

Break up the chickpeas and pieces of potato to thicken it slightly. Season carefully with sea salt and freshly ground black pepper, and pour into hot bowls. Top with a splash of olive oil and some grated Parmesan cheese.

Cannellini Bean and Smoked Haddock Soup

Soups should come from a pan and not a carton or can. Using cooked beans saves on preparation time but you can soak some dried beans in water overnight if you would like and then cook for an hour or two in boiling water until tender. I have made this soup from start to finish in 20 minutes. Use a powerful blender such as a KitchenAid for that velvety smooth restaurant finish.

Serves 4

a knob of butter
2 large onions, sliced
1 x 400g cannellini/haricot beans,
drained and rinsed
800ml light Chicken Stock (see page 14)
a pinch of saffron, soaked in hot water
250ml whipping cream
250g smoked haddock, skin and bones
discarded
Tabasco sauce

Melt the butter in a heavy saucepan, add the onions and cook until soft. Add the beans, stock, saffron and cream and bring to a gentle simmer. Add the haddock and cook for 5–10 minutes. Transfer in small batches to a powerful liquidiser and blitz until smooth. Pass it though a fine sieve and pour it into a clean pan.

Reheat and then adjust the seasoning, adding a good warming splash of Tabasco. Garnish with fingers of toasted rustic bread.

Pasta and Potato Soup/Pasta e Patate

At home, this soup was made religiously every Friday. We strictly kept the Catholic tradition of not eating meat on Fridays. This was no great hardship as pasta e patate is one of the most satisfying, comforting soups on the face of the earth. No matter what the priest says, no Italian mother would willingly deprive her family. In practice, the rule was obeyed in spirit only.

Serves 4

2 tbsp extra virgin olive oil
1 garlic clove
1 small piece peperoncino (dried chilli)
1 onion, very finely chopped
1 x 400g can Italian plum tomatoes
1.75 litres hot water
2 floury potatoes, peeled and diced
salt to taste
a handful of ditali rigate pasta (or small chunky pasta)
freshly grated Parmesan

Warm the oil in a large thick-bottomed saucepan and add the garlic and chilli. Add the chopped onion, stir and coat with the oil. Put the lid on and cook the onion slowly until it is soft and translucent. Don't let it burn.

Whizz the tomatoes in a liquidiser and, if you can be bothered, strain out the seeds by pressing the purée through a sieve. (You can use tomato passata instead.) Add the sieved tomatoes and 1 litre of the water to the onion, along with the potatoes

and 1 tsp salt. Cover and cook for 30 minutes or so until the potatoes have softened. Remove the garlic.

Add the remaining water and the pasta. Stir and simmer for 10 minutes until the pasta is al dente. Check the seasoning, and serve in big warm bowls with plenty of freshly grated Parmesan.

I often poach a couple of eggs in this soup. When the pasta has started to cook, break 1–2 eggs on to the surface and let them poach gently as the pasta finishes cooking.

(From *Dear Francesca*, Ebury Press, 2002)

White Bean and Carrot Soup

This is extremely heartening and comforting.

Serves 4

500g haricot beans, soaked for 3-4 hours and drained
1 small bunch parsley
4 garlic cloves, peeled
1 ripe tomato, halved
500g carrots, peeled and finely sliced
3 tbsp extra virgin olive oil
1.25 litres Chicken Stock (see page 14)
salt and pepper to taste
4 thin slices toasted sourdough, rye or
country-style bread

Boil the soaked beans in plenty of fresh unsalted water with the parsley stalks (keep the leaves), 2 of the garlic cloves, crushed, and the tomato halves, until the beans are al dente, about 30-45 minutes. Drain.

Coarsely chop the remaining garlic and fry with the carrots in 2 tbsp of the olive oil for 2-3 minutes over a medium high heat, stirring occasionally. Add the cooked beans, chicken stock and the coarsely chopped parsley leaves, and simmer for 20 minutes.

Remove half the beans and purée them, then return them to the pot, stir to mix and season with sea salt and cracked black pepper.

Grill the bread and put one slice in the bottom of each bowl. Drizzle over the remaining olive oil, season with sea salt, and spoon over the hot soup.

Garlic, Chorizo and Chickpea Broth with Egg Noodles

The hearty flavour of pimentón-flavoured chorizo really lifts this hearty soup, and the 'noodles' are really easy to make.

Serves 6–8

12 garlic cloves, halved
80ml extra virgin olive oil
200g chorizo sausage
2 large red onions, diced
1 tbsp fresh rosemary leaves, roughly chopped
1 tbsp fresh oregano leaves, roughly chopped
600g canned chickpeas, drained and rinsed
2 bay leaves
finely grated zest and juice of 1 lemon
1 litre Chicken or Vegetable Stock
(see pages 14 or 12)

Noodles

1 egg
2 tsp cold water
2 pinches salt
1 tsp olive oil

Cook the garlic in the oil in a very small pan over a very gentle heat, stirring occasionally, until soft and golden (about 20 minutes). Remove with a slotted spoon. Peel any casing from the chorizo and slice half into thin discs, then fry until cooked in the same oil that you cooked the garlic in. Remove with a slotted spoon and set aside. Cut the remaining chorizo into small cubes.

Transfer the oil to a larger pot. Add the onions, diced chorizo, rosemary and oregano, and fry until they begin to caramelise. Add the caramelised garlic, the chickpeas, bay leaves, lemon zest and stock and bring to the boil. Simmer for 30 minutes.

Make the noodles while the soup is cooking. Lightly beat together the egg, water and salt. Heat a 24cm non-stick pan and brush with a few drops of oil. Drizzle in the egg mixture so it covers the base of the pan. Cook over a moderate heat until just set. Tip on to a board, roll up and cut into 1cm slices. Unroll into 'noodles'.

Taste the broth for seasoning and stir in the lemon juice. Ladle into bowls and serve with the egg noodles and chorizo discs scattered on top.

(From *A World in My Kitchen*, Moa Beckett, Hodder, 2003)

Yoghurt Soup with Rice

Apart from the pleasure it gives, soup represents to me homely comfort food, affection and nurture. In this Turkish soup, the egg yolk and flour prevent the yoghurt from curdling. The rice is best cooked separately and added in at the end as it gets bloated and mushy if left in the soup too long.

Serves 6
100g basmati rice
salt and pepper to taste
1.2 litres Chicken Stock (see page 14, but you may use 2 stock cubes)
450g thick strained yoghurt
2 tbsp plain flour
2 egg yolks
1½ tbsp dried mint
1 x 400g can chickpeas, drained and rinsed (optional)
30g butter or 2 tbsp olive oil (optional)
2 tsp paprika (optional)

Cook the rice in boiling salted water until tender, and drain.

Bring the chicken stock to the boil in a large pan.

In a bowl beat the yoghurt with the flour and egg yolks until blended, then add the mint, salt and pepper. Pour this into the stock, stirring vigorously. Continue to stir, over a very low heat, until the soup thickens slightly.

Before serving, add the rice and chickpeas (if using) and heat through. If you like, heat the butter or olive oil, stir in the paprika and dribble a little of this over each serving.

Variations

A pinch of saffron strands steeped in 2 tbsp hot water may be added instead of the butter and paprika at the end.

An Iranian version adds a ¼ tsp of turmeric and a variety of chopped herbs, including parsley, tarragon and chives, as well as shredded spinach.

Acknowledgements

Thank you to the following chefs and food writers who contributed recipes to this collection:

Galton Blackiston, Antonio Carluccio, Sam and Sam Clark, Tom Conran, Mary Contini, Jill Dupleix, Hugh Fearnley-Whittingstall, Peter Gordon, Henry Harris, Angela Hartnett, Fergus Henderson, Mark Hix, Nigella Lawson, Faith MacArthur, Jamie Oliver, Bruce Poole, Gordon Ramsay, Gary Rhodes, Claudia Roden, Delia Smith, John Torode

The Charities
Our aim in compiling *Soup Kitchen* and the *Little Book of Soup* is to raise funds for charities which care about and act on homelessness in the UK. Rather than reinforcing stereotypes of soup and homelessness, we hope that this book will translate a widespread contemporary interest in food and healthy living into funds for invaluable short-term and long-term homeless projects.

70% of all money raised from sales of the *Little Book of Soup* and all related promotional activities will be donated to charities who work to support homeless people in London and around the UK.

Our main beneficiaries include:

The Salvation Army
Registered Charity No. 214779
www.salvationarmy.org.uk
T 0845 634 0101

Centrepoint
Registered Charity No. 292411
www.centrepoint.org.uk
T 0207 426 5300

For further information on the work of all charities involved with *Soup Kitchen* and fundraising activities and progress, please see www.soupkitchen.org.uk.

Index